Hello Kitty®
FUN DOODLES

CREATE AND C... SUPERCUTE ...

RP | KIDS
PHILADELPHIA • LONDON

9 8 7 6 5 4 3 2 1
Digit on the right indicates the number of this printing

Library of Congress Control Number: 2009943430

ISBN 978-0-7624-3821-1

Cover and interior design by Frances J. Soo Ping Chow
Written and edited by Jordana Tusman
Typography: Chowderhead, Funnybone, and Univers

Published by Running Press Kids, an imprint of
Running Press Book Publishers
2300 Chestnut Street
Philadelphia, PA 19103-4371

Visit us on the web!
www.runningpress.com
www.sanrio.com

Hello Kitty is doodling.
Can you help her doodle hearts and rainbows?

Hello Kitty and her friends are playing baseball.
Can you draw the bases and the rest of her friends on the field?

Hello Kitty is riding her bike with her twin sister Mimmy.
Draw the friends they see on their bike ride.

Hello Kitty and her family are camping in their backyard.
Can you draw their tent? Draw Mimmy roasting marshmallows.

Hello Kitty and Mimmy are picking flowers.
How many flowers can you draw in the grass?

Hello Kitty and Jodie are juggling. Jodie is juggling bouncy balls. What is Hello Kitty juggling?

Hello Kitty is dancing.
Can you draw her friends dancing with her?

JUKEBOX
3 Hits 25¢

BURGERS
w/FRIES
50¢

35¢
SUNDAES

Hello Kitty is fishing in her little boat with Dear Daniel.
Can you draw the fish they've caught?
Do you see fish in the water?

Hello Kitty is making pictures in the art studio with Thomas.
What have they painted today on their canvases?

Hello Kitty is sewing a dress for Fifi.
What color is Fifi's new dress? Can you draw
clothes in the wardrobe?

Hello Kitty is at the beach.
What creatures do you see in the ocean?

Hello Kitty is walking dogs.
Draw dogs on the ends of the leashes.

Hello Kitty is at a picnic.
Draw the food they are eating today.

Mama is reading a book to Hello Kitty before they go to sleep.
What other books are on Hello Kitty's bookshelf?

Hello Kitty is at school. What is the lesson on the chalkboard?
Draw students and what you see on their desks.

Hello Kitty is playing in the snow.
Can you draw Hello Kitty making a snowman?

Hello Kitty is drinking a milkshake at the malt shop.
Can you draw Hello Kitty's friends next to her?

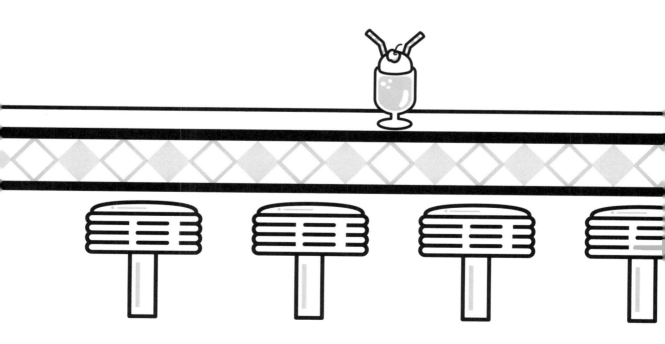

Hello Kitty and Mimmy are playing at the park.
Draw the animals they see.

Hello Kitty is celebrating Joey's birthday. Can you draw a delicious
cake and other food on the table?

Hello Kitty and Grandpa are building forts with pillows and blankets.
Can you help them build a fort?

Hello Kitty is playing outside.
Can you draw bugs and flowers?

Hello Kitty is playing hopscotch and jump rope with Fifi.
Can you draw the squares and fill in the numbers?
Can you draw Fifi with her jump rope?

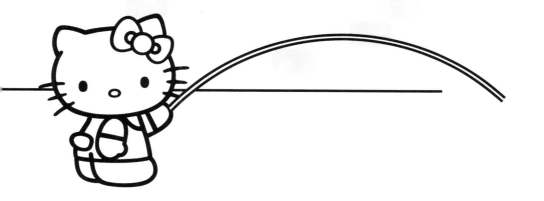

Hello Kitty is sledding.
Draw all of Hello Kitty's friends sledding
next to her down the hill.

Hello Kitty is eating dinner with her family.
What did they cook?

Hello Kitty is eating dessert. Can you draw ice cream scoops on top of the ice cream cones? Don't forget the toppings!

Hello Kitty and her friends are at the circus.
Can you draw Fifi sitting on top of the elephant and
Lorry making balloon animals?

Hello Kitty and Joey are going on a balloon ride.
Can you draw what they see?

Hello Kitty and Tippy are playing in Tippy's treehouse.
Can you decorate the treehouse?

Hello Kitty and Tippy are going home on the school bus.
Draw Papa waiting for her at the bus stop.

Hello Kitty is picking apples from trees.
Can you draw apples for Hello Kitty to pick?

Hello Kitty and her friends are playing hide-and-seek.
Can you draw them hiding in the house?

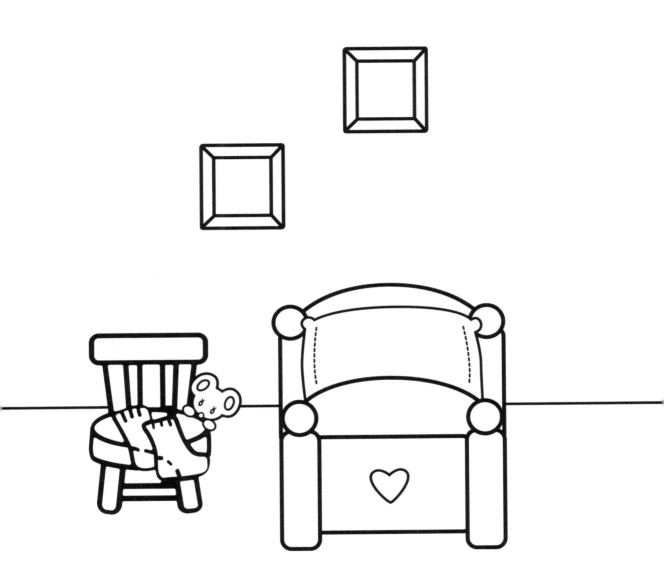

Hello Kitty and Mimmy are playing with their stuffed animals.
Can you draw stuffed animals on their bookshelves?

Hello Kitty is having a bath.
Draw some toys and bubbles for her to play with.

Hello Kitty is going on a safari. Draw some of the wild animals that she sees on her trip. Design a safari postcard for her to send to her friends.

Hello Kitty and Grandma are at the museum and looking at the paintings. Can you draw paintings on the wall?

Hello Kitty is playing in the rain.
Draw Hello Kitty in her rain gear.

HELLO KITTY'S ROOM

Hello Kitty and her friends are having a slumber party.
Draw Hello Kitty and her friends in their sleeping bags.

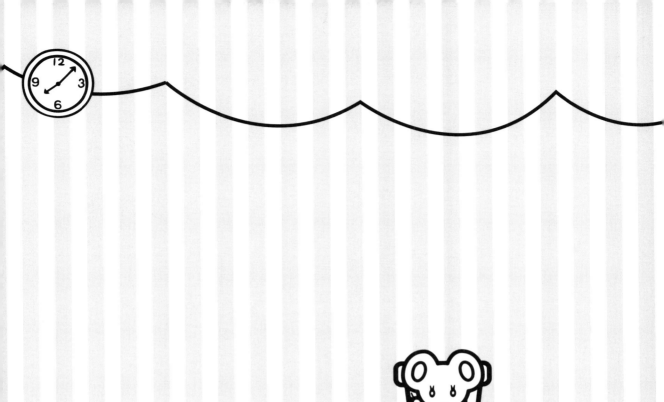

Hello Kitty is eating cookies that Mimmy baked.
Can you draw and decorate the cookies?

Hello Kitty is flying a kite.
Can you draw a kite on the end of the string?

Thanks for playing with Hello Kitty and her friends!
Can you draw a picture of yourself with your best friends?